Evelyn Waugh

by

DAVID LODGE

 *Columbia University Press*

NEW YORK & LONDON 1971

COLUMBIA ESSAYS ON MODERN WRITERS
is a series of critical studies of English,
Continental, and other writers whose works are of contemporary
artistic and intellectual significance.

Editor

William York Tindall

Advisory Editors

Jacques Barzun   W. T. H. Jackson   Joseph A. Mazzeo

Evelyn Waugh is Number 58 of the series

DAVID LODGE
is Senior Lecturer in English at the University of
Birmingham. He is the author of *Language of Fiction*,
Graham Greene (in this series), and several novels.

To Elsie Duncan-Jones

Copyright © 1971 Columbia University Press
I S B N: 0–231–03258–7
Library of Congress Catalog Card Number: 78–136497
Printed in the United States of America

Acknowledgment is made to Chapman & Hall for permission
to quote from the works of Evelyn Waugh and to Little,
Brown and Company for permission to quote from
Decline and Fall (copyright 1928, 1929 by Evelyn Waugh).

Evelyn Waugh

It may happen in the next hundred years that the English novelists of the present day will come to be valued as we now value the artists and craftsmen of the late eighteenth century. The originators, the exuberant men, are extinct and in their place subsists and modestly flourishes a generation notable for elegance and variety of contrivance. . . . Among these novelists Mr. Gilbert Pinfold stood quite high.

Thus begins Evelyn Waugh's *The Ordeal of Gilbert Pinfold* (1957), a work so transparently autobiographical that we must regard the passage as some kind of exercise in self-definition. Out of context, "the originators, the exuberant men" might be taken to refer to writers like James Joyce and D. H. Lawrence. Read this way, the passage confirms the orthodox view of literary critics, that a reaction occurred in English fiction of the thirties and subsequent decades, against the "modern" or "experimental" novel, leading to a certain decline in creative ambition and achievement. Readers aware of Mr. Pinfold-Waugh's well-advertised distaste for the modern in life and art will, however, suspect that in this passage he was more likely to be thinking of Dickens than Joyce, and that it was against the nineteenth-century masters rather than their twentieth-century successors that he modestly measured himself. In fact, either interpretation would be somewhat misleading. It is true that, in 1962, Waugh replied to an interviewer's question: "Experiment! God forbid! Look at the results of experiment in . . . Joyce. He started off writing very well, then you can watch him going mad with

[3]

vanity." And it is true that the salient characteristics of Waugh's own work—his carefully constructed plots, his lucid, classically correct prose, his abundant and instantly accessible humor—seem to have little in common with the tortured and tortuous products of modernism. Nevertheless, Evelyn Waugh's fiction, particularly his early fiction, has a definable, though oblique, continuity with the modern movement in literature. To try and define it is to risk taking up an incongruously solemn stance toward a writer chiefly—and rightly—admired for his comic gifts; but the risk is worth taking if it helps to explain the difference between Waugh and, say, P. G. Wodehouse. Waugh is indeed wonderfully entertaining, but he is more than an entertainer.

In an early (1929) uncollected essay on Ronald Firbank, that late-flowering bloom of the Decadence whose satirical romances of aristocratic and ecclesiastical manners influenced him deeply, Waugh commended Firbank for never forgetting that "the novel should be directed for entertainment"; but the burden of his argument is Firbank's importance as a technical innovator:

He achieved a new, balanced interrelation of subject and form. Nineteenth-century novelists achieved a balance only by complete submission to the idea of the succession of events in an arbitrarily limited period of time . . . the novelist was fettered by the chain of cause and effect. . . . [Firbank's] late novels are almost wholly devoid of any attributions of cause to effect; there is the barest minimum of direct description; his compositions are built up, intricately and with a balanced alternation of the wildest extravagances and the most austere economy, with conversational *nuances.*

The relevance of this account to Waugh's own early novels will be apparent to anyone familiar with them. In the novels Firbank published through the twenties, the young Waugh found the model for a kind of fiction that could be distinctively modern without surrendering to what has been called "the fallacy of expressive form." Since modern man inhabits a universe that seems confused, fragmented, lacking in order and stability, therefore it is inevitable that his art should display equivalent formal characteristics: so runs the orthodox defense of modern art. Waugh, while sharing this view of modern secular civilization, declined, for reasons that were partly aesthetic, partly temperamental, and partly philosophical, to follow the advice of Conrad's Stein, "In the destructive element immerse," or to pursue, as did Eliot, Pound, Joyce, and Virginia Woolf, the verbal imitation of a disorderly universe. It is clearly of these latter writers that Waugh is thinking when he writes, of "other solutions" to the problem Firbank solved, that "in them the author has been forced into a subjective attitude to his material; Firbank remained objective." So did Waugh. The disorderliness, the contingency, the collapse of value and meaning in contemporary life, are rendered dramatically through conversational nuances and ironic juxtaposition of scenes; narratively through the elimination or parody of cause and effect (events in Waugh's novels are either gratuitous or grotesquely disproportionate to their causes). But the implied author mediating this vision of comic anarchy remains objective—morally, emotionally, and (perhaps most important) stylistically. He does not, except in passages of obvious pastiche, bend his verbal medium to fit the contours of his characters' sensibility, nor dissolve the structure of formal English prose to imitate subconscious or unconscious processes. He retains always a classical detachment, lucidity, and poise. This is the source of Evelyn Waugh's distinctive tone, and of his most characteristic comic effects; it is also what troubles the critics who have accused him of being cruel, snobbish, and nihilistic.

[5]

For contemporary readers the modernity of Waugh's early novels was partly a function of his instinct for the symptoms of social and cultural change, particularly as it affected the upper classes. His crystalline comedies reflected back to them images, at once glamorous and grotesque, of what was distinctively new in their experience: air travel and fancy dress, cocktails and chromium plating, motor-racing and movie-making. He was one of the first novelists to grasp the significance of the telephone in modern life and to exploit it extensively in fiction. In at least one case he created rather than imitated fashion, putting the "sick-making," "shy-making" slang of his own coterie into general currency with *Vile Bodies* (1930). Yet these early novels have not seemed, in the pejorative sense, "dated" to subsequent generations of readers, partly because the topical detail is handled with such wit and economy, and partly because it is made to serve a larger literary meaning. For this last I should like to adopt a term used by Professor Northrop Frye in his monograph on T. S. Eliot: the "myth of decline."

The myth of decline is as old as man's nostalgia for a pastoral paradise lost, but it acquires a special importance in nineteenth- and twentieth-century literature, which, as Frye points out, has tended to invert the Enlightenment graph of human history as an upward curve of inevitable Progress, and to point instead to an accelerating deterioration in the quality of life. The beginning of the decline (or Second Fall) is variously located in the Industrial Revolution, the English Civil War, the Reformation, the birth of Christianity, or man's first departure from primitive tribal life, but the historical provenance of the idea is less important than its imaginative power—hence the appropriateness of the term "myth."

That Evelyn Waugh nourished his own version of this myth was signaled by the title of his first novel, *Decline and Fall*

(1928). Clearly inapplicable to the hero, Paul Pennyfeather, whose fortunes follow a circular rather than a vertical trajectory, the title conveys a judgment on the society which shocks, seduces, dazzles, and exploits him during his hectic sortie beyond the walls of Scone College. Obviously, it echoes Gibbon's *Decline and Fall of the Roman Empire*, a work which Waugh perhaps read as a student of History at Oxford, and with which he seems to have had a kind of negative identification. As sly allusions to Gibbon in *Helena* (1950) make clear, Waugh deplored the historian's Enlightenment skepticism and anticlericalism, but admired his style—an elegant, urbane, sardonic style that was evidently one of the models for his own. Thus we may speculate that Evelyn Waugh saw himself as chronicling—not discursively, but imaginatively, not retrospectively, but immediately—the decline and fall of another great Empire and the culture associated with it. Certainly the title "Decline and Fall" would be as appropriate to any of his other novels as it is to his first.

"'Change and decay in all around I see,'" sings Uncle Theodore, in *Scoop* (1938), gazing out of the morning-room window of Boot Magna Hall at the immense trees that

had suffered, some from ivy, some from lightning, some from the various malignant disorders that vegetation is heir to, but all principally from old age. Some were supported with trusses and crutches of iron, some were filled with cement; some even now, in June, could show only a handful of green leaves at their extremities. Sap ran thin and slow; a gusty night always brought down a litter of dead timber.

The trees in the park reflect the state of the human inhabitants of the Hall, a family of ancient and noble lineage now enjoying neither modern comforts nor traditional dignity, its energy and resources almost entirely absorbed by the lavish maintenance of an army of aged and bedridden servants. The country

[7]

house as an image of decline and decay can be traced right through Waugh's *œuvre:* King's Thursday in *Decline and Fall*, demolished to make way for Dr. Otto Silenus's "surprising creation of ferro-concrete and aluminium"; Doubting Hall in *Vile Bodies*, dilapidated seat of Colonel Blount, whose footmen were killed in the war and whose butler suffers terribly in his feet; obsolescent Hetton Abbey in *A Handful of Dust* (1934), itself a Victorian supplanter of a genuine old house; and all the fine houses, including Brideshead, of *Brideshead Revisited* (1945) that are despoiled, abused, or demolished almost before the narrator has time to record them in "Ryder's English Homes."

In *Edmund Campion* (1935), a biography of the English recusant martyr published five years after Waugh's conversion to the Roman Catholic faith, he expounded a historical version of his myth of decline which can be traced back through Chesterton, Belloc, and Tawney to Cobbett and Lingard. In this perspective, the Reformation was a catastrophe which stifled at birth the "spacious, luminous world of Catholic humanism" personified in Thomas More, and left England, at the end of the Tudor dynasty, with a future of "competitive nationalism, competitive industrialism, competitive imperialism . . . the power and the weakness of great possessions." It is significant, however, that this Catholic humanism, the union of all that is best in religious and secular culture, was admittedly a possibility rather than a fact: in Waugh's historical scheme there is no point at which all was right with the world. Perfection exists outside time and space altogether, in the Kingdom of God.

Translated into political terms, such a view can only be described as conservative and reactionary; and Waugh's qualified support of Mussolini and Franco in the thirties was predictable, if ill-judged. In time, Waugh recognized that his values and beliefs had no place in the field of practical politics. Mr. Pinfold is described as professing "an idiosyncratic tory-ism which was quite unrepresented in the political parties of his time," and Waugh himself advertised the fact that he had never voted in a Parliamentary election, once parrying a challenge on this point by saying that he did not presume to advise his Sovereign on her choice of ministers. The riposte was characteristic and revealing. There is an element of self-indulgent fantasy, of role-playing, in Waugh's myth of decline, as he seems to concede on occasion—in, for instance, John Plant's comment, in *Work Suspended* (1942), on his generation's cult of domestic architecture:

When the poetic mood was on us, we turned to buildings and gave them that place which our fathers accorded to Nature—to almost any buildings, but particularly those in the classical tradition, and, more particularly, in its decay. It was a kind of nostalgia for the style of living which we emphatically rejected in practical affairs.

In a similar way, Evelyn Waugh's imagination is more quickly fired by institutions in an advanced stage of decay than in their putative prime. The artist in Waugh seizes with glee upon what the educated Catholic gentleman most deplores, a process perfectly exemplified by Dennis Barlow's rapturous exploration of Hollywood's monstrous cemetery in *The Loved One* (1948): "His interest was no longer purely technical nor purely satiric. In a zone of insecurity in the mind where none but the artist dare trespass, the tribes were gathering." Not surprisingly Evelyn Waugh was one of the earliest and most sophisticated exponents of that form of taste known as "camp" (see, for instance, his deliciously ambivalent appreciation of Gaudi's architecture in *Labels* [1930]).

When culture is seen as a process of continual decline, nothing is invulnerable to irony. The modern is ridiculed by contrast with the traditional, but attempts to maintain or restore the traditional in the face of change are also seen as ridiculous; and in any case the traditional usually turns out to be in some way false or compromised. This can be clearly seen by retracing the "house" motif in Waugh's work. Consider, for example, Paul Pennyfeather's approach to King's Thursday:

"English spring," thought Paul. "In the dreaming ancestral beauty of the English country." Surely, he thought, these great chestnuts in the morning sun stood for something enduring and serene in a world that had lost its reason and would so stand when the chaos and confusion were forgotten? And surely it was the spirit of William Morris that whispered to him in Margot Beste-Chetwynde's motor-car about seed-time and the harvest, the superb succession of the seasons, the harmonious interdependence of rich and poor, of dignity, innocence and tradition? But at a turn in the drive, the cadence of his thoughts was abruptly transected. They had come into sight of the house.

"Golly," said Beste-Chetwynde. "Mamma has done herself proud this time."

Obviously Paul's reverie has the effect of highlighting the incongruity and perversity of the new Bauhaus-style King's Thursday. But the joke rebounds upon Paul's reverie, which is exposed as a sentimental illusion, compromisingly enjoyed from the comfort of a modern motor-car, derived second-hand from literary sources and revealing an immature desire to escape chaos and confusion. The case of Hetton in *A Handful of Dust* is similar: though its Victorian neo-Gothic is marginally preferable to the white chromium-plating and natural sheepskin in which Mrs. Beaver proposes to "do over" one of its rooms, we are left in no doubt that it is a hideously ugly fake. Tony Last's devotion to it, though touching, is misdirected, a symptom and a symbol of his innocence and immaturity. In *Brideshead Revisited*, it is true, we find something more like an orthodox conservationist attitude—the myth of decline has become more rigid and polemical here—but at the very end, the narrator recognizes that the disfigurement of Brideshead by its military occupants and the dispersal of the aristocratic family that once occupied it matter less than the fact that the sanctuary lamp continues to burn in the ugly little *art nouveau* chapel.

The myth of decline provided Evelyn Waugh with a sliding scale of value on which almost everything is found in some way defective. The only absolute to which he appeals —the ideal of Christian perfection—is not on the scale of secular history at all. Thus he was being quite consistent, though no doubt deliberately provocative, when he said late in life that he saw nothing objectionable in the total destruction of the world providing it came about, as seemed likely, accidentally (that is, without sin being committed). He has been accused of being less consistent in his later fiction—of speciously identifying the eternal verities with a particular human social group, the English Catholic aristocracy and gentry. Of his earlier novels, where the absolute values of Christianity are not explicitly invoked, it has been said that they lack a moral center: that the modern and the traditional, civilization and barbarism, and every shade of political thought and racial prejudice are rendered absurd by being played off against each other rather than measured against positive norms. Waugh himself has encouraged this view by disowning the title of satirist in these terms:

Satire is a matter of period. It flourishes in a stable society and presupposes homogeneous moral standards—the early Roman Empire and eighteenth-century Europe. It is aimed at inconsistency and hypocrisy. It exposes polite cruelty and folly by exaggerating them. All this has no place in the century of the Common Man, where vice no longer pays lip service to virtue.

This remark is as confusing as it is revealing. There is indeed satire written from clear, commonly shared principles, but we do not have to look beyond the eighteenth century to find quite another kind of satire. No one has satisfactorily identified the positive principles behind *The Tale of a Tub* or the Fourth Book of *Gulliver's Travels*. Yet these works certainly have the motives and effects attributed to satire by Waugh—and so do his own early novels. It would seem that when the satiric impulse is joined to the fictive imagination and the comic spirit, as it is in Swift and Waugh, an imaginative energy is released too strong to be contained within a simple didactic framework. The artist begins almost playfully to explore the possibilities of his *donnée*, and the reader is invited to respond to a mosaic of local comic and satiric effects rather than laboriously to decode a consistent message. The anchor of the reader's response will in this case be, not an abstractable set of positive values, but the intelligence and poise of the implied author as conveyed by his style and management of events. There *is*, in fact, behind Waugh's fictional world, a consistent point of view—that of a dogmatic Christian antihumanism; but it is not one with which the reader has to identify in order to enjoy the satirical comedy.

Evelyn Arthur St. John Waugh was born on October 28, 1903, in a modest villa in the London suburb of Hampstead, and died in 1966, the owner of Combe Florey House, near Taunton in Somerset. Both his parents came from respectable upper-middle class families of professional standing. His father, Arthur Waugh, was a publisher (director, in fact, of Evelyn's own publishers, Chapman and Hall), a journalist, and a minor critic. In the readable but somewhat guarded autobiography of his early years, *A Little Learning* (1964), Evelyn described his father as "a Man of Letters . . . a category, like the maiden aunt, that is now almost extinct." If the portraits of Mr. Plant, Sr. and Mr. Ryder, Sr. are any guide, Arthur Waugh cultivated his own obsolescence with a certain relish, and thus indirectly nourished his son's myth of decline.

[12]

Evelyn seems to have enjoyed a tranquil, happy childhood, overshadowed in more ways than one by his elder brother, Alec. After leaving Sherborne, Mr. Waugh's beloved old school, under something of a cloud, Alec precociously dashed off a novel about his experiences there. *The Loom of Youth*, published in 1917 when its author was serving in the trenches of Flanders, attracted considerable attention, particularly for the (then) startling candor with which it treated adolescent homosexuality. Such was the notoriety of this book that Evelyn was unable to follow his brother to Sherborne, and was sent instead to Lancing, a school of Anglican ecclesiastical temper that his parents thought suitable for a child of rather exceptional piety. It was at Lancing, however, that Evelyn became an agnostic; he was better known there as the founder of the Dilettanti Society and the Corpse Club. In 1922 he went up to Hertford College, Oxford, to read History.

To be a child or adolescent during a major war is inevitably to feel diminished and frustrated, and for Evelyn this feeling must have been personalized in the glamorous figure of his brother, Alec (who went on to become a writer of popular novels and travel books). It is not surprising, therefore, that at Oxford Evelyn felt, in his own words, "reborn into full youth." By 1922, the sober veterans of the war had departed, and the University was "re-possessed by the young." The manner of their repossession—the drinking, the ragging, the dandyism, the defiance of authority, the experimentation with every style of life and art—is unforgettably evoked, for all its nostalgic idealization, in the long first section of *Brideshead Revisited*. Waugh later described his own undergraduate career as "idle, dissolute and extravagant." It ended inauspiciously in 1924 with a third class result in his final examinations. "My education, it seems to me," he wrote, "was the preparation for one trade only, that of an English prose writer," but it was six years before he discovered his vocation. In the intervening time he enrolled for a while at an art school, took teaching posts in two private schools, was a probationary reporter on the *Daily Express,* and even, bizarrely, contemplated apprenticeship to a carpenter. All this experience was to yield fruit later, but at the time Waugh was far from happy: *A Little Learning* leaves him in 1925 lugubriously contemplating suicide on a Welsh beach. In 1927, however, he obtained a commission from Duckworth's to write a biography of Dante Gabriel Rossetti, and became engaged to Evelyn Gardner, daughter of Lord Burghclere. He seems to have written *Decline and Fall* in a desperate attempt to convince his fiancée's skeptical parents that he was capable of earning his living as a writer. *Rossetti,* published in May, 1928, was kindly received, and was indeed a very creditable first book, displaying the elegance, economy, and wit that were to mark Waugh's subsequent writing. *Decline and Fall,* published by Chapman and Hall in the autumn of 1928, after Duckworth's had rejected it as being too risqué, was a definite success. The two Evelyns were married clandestinely that summer, and the following winter accepted, as a delayed honeymoon, the offer of a free Mediterranean cruise in return for discreet advertisement of the shipping line in the resulting travel book, *Labels* (1930). On their return to England in the spring of 1929, Waugh retired to the country to write *Vile Bodies* in solitude. In the summer, his wife informed him that she was in love with another man, and the couple separated. Civil divorce proceedings were begun, and Waugh resumed *Vile Bodies.* It was published in January, 1930, and at the same time Waugh informed his friend Christopher Hollis that he was receiving instruction in the Roman Catholic faith from the Jesuits. He was received into the Church in the summer of that year. Thus, the years between 1927 and 1930 encompassed three fateful and closely connected events in Waugh's life: his self-discovery as a literary artist, the breakdown of his first marriage, and his conversion to Catholicism.

In *Labels*, Waugh describes the experience of "looping the loop" in one of the early aircraft:

In "looping," the aeroplane shoots steeply upwards until the sensation becomes unendurable and one knows that in another moment it will turn completely over. Then it keeps on shooting up and does turn completely over. One looks down into an unfathomable abyss of sky, while over one's head a great umbrella of fields and houses has suddenly opened. Then one shuts one's eyes. My companion on this occasion was a large-hearted and reckless man; he was President of the Union, logical, matter-of-fact in disposition, inclined towards beer and Ye Olde Merrie Englande. . . . He had come with me in order to assure himself that it was all really nonsense about things heavier than air being able to fly. He sat behind me throughout, muttering, "Oh, my God, oh, Christ, oh, my God." On the way back he scarcely spoke, and two days later, without a word to anyone, he was received into the Roman Church.

This is not merely a funny story, told with Waugh's usual finesse. It is also a parable. Twenty years later, writing about his conversion to Catholicism, Evelyn Waugh said: "Those who have read my works will perhaps understand the character of the world into which I exuberantly launched myself. Ten years of that world sufficed to show me that life there, or anywhere, was unintelligible and unendurable without God." Stephen Greenblatt has shrewdly observed the occurrence in Waugh's fiction of the demonic imagery of circles, wheels, and spirals that Northrop Frye associates with satire and irony, pointing to the circular construction of many of Waugh's plots, and to such motifs as the "Great Wheel at Luna Park" in *Decline and Fall*, and Agatha Runcible's nightmare as she is dying from her motor-racing exploit ("I thought we were all going round and round in a motor race and none of us could stop") in *Vile Bodies*. To these examples we may add the "unendurable" sensation of looping the loop. All are images of the accelerating collapse of order and meaning which many artists perceived in Western culture and society after the trauma of World War I.

> Things fall apart; the centre cannot hold;
> Mere anarchy is loosed upon the world.

The traditional resources of Merrie England were clearly inadequate to this sense of crisis. Many of Waugh's contemporaries turned for salvation to Marx and political commitment; he followed the example of his fellow passenger and joined the most uncompromisingly dogmatic Christian church, still, in those days, unshaken by the winds of secular change. No doubt the decision was precipitated by the abrupt breakdown of his marriage. This is the opinion of his brother, Alec, to whom he said at the time, "The trouble about the world today is that there's not enough religion in it. There's nothing to stop young people from doing whatever they feel like doing at the moment." The experience was obviously bitter and profound in its effects: in novel after novel the theme of sexual infidelity—usually of a woman, usually revealed with shattering unexpectedness—recurs. Yet the flat, if understandable moralism of Evelyn's remark to his brother rarely intrudes into the fiction, not even into *Vile Bodies*, written in the midst of this domestic crisis. In *Decline and Fall*, written two years earlier, we find only hints of the way his mind was beginning to turn, hidden beneath the surface of what is in many ways his most stylized and high-spirited essay in comedy.

It begins with two Oxford dons cowering in their rooms, anticipating with relish the fines they will be able to impose as a result of the celebrations of the Bollinger Society that are in progress.

[16]

A shriller note could now be heard rising from Sir Alastair's rooms: any who have heard that sound will shrink at the recollection of it; it is the sound of the English county families baying for broken glass. . . . "It'll be more if they attack the Chapel," said Mr Sniggs. "Oh, please God, make them attack the Chapel."

The comic inversion of natural or traditional order implied in the transmutation of huntsmen into hounds and prayers offered for sacrilege is unflaggingly sustained in the sequel. The Bollingerites escape lightly compared to Paul Penny-feather, an earnest and respectable scholar whom they intercept cycling home from a meeting of the League of Nations Union and deprive of his trousers, in consequence of which he is expelled from the college. The episode and its aftermath are related in a few rapid, cross-cut scenes in which everyone is very civil but entirely indifferent to the monstrous injustice suffered by Paul. Even Paul's own indignation is deliberately retarded till the very end of the chapter, when he tips the college porter; and then it is qualified by an unexpected adverbial phrase (a characteristic device of Waugh's):

"Well, goodbye, Blackall," he said. "I don't suppose I shall see you again for some time."
"No, sir, and very sorry I am to hear about it. I expect you'll be becoming a schoolmaster, sir. That's what most of the gentlemen does, sir, that gets sent down for indecent behaviour."
"God damn and blast them all to hell," said Paul meekly to himself as he drove to the station, and then he felt rather ashamed, because he rarely swore.

Paul, as has often been observed, is a Candide figure, whose innocence is used as a foil for the exposure of folly and vice in the world at large. True to the porter's prediction, he is compelled to take employment as a schoolmaster at Llanabba Castle, an outrageously fraudulent establishment presided over by Augustus Fagan, Esq., Ph.D. Here he meets three characters each of whom, without being heavily symbolic, has something to tell him about Life. His colleague Mr. Prendergast, an ex-clergyman afflicted with Doubts, is a cautionary example of what happens when spirituality is divorced from dogma. The baffling lies and impostures of the butler, Philbrick, caricature the bewildering social mobility of postwar society. Grimes, another teacher, is more complex, and his significance more of a riddle. In one sense he embodies the decline of the public-school code which he so brazenly exploits ("I should think," he says, "I've been put on my feet more often than any living man"); in another his infinitely elastic, totally amoral capacity for survival compels respect, and under his tuition Paul becomes a little less innocent.

The Llanabba School Sports forms the backdrop to a hilarious comedy of incompatible manners between the academic staff, the uncouth Welsh natives, and the visiting parents, among whom is the glamorous Mrs. Margot Beste-Chetwynde. Paul falls in love with Margot, and eagerly accepts an invitation to accompany her son to King's Thursday. There, after a highly unconventional house party has dispersed, he is astonished and delighted to find his affection reciprocated—and indeed consummated. Margot proposes marriage, and while the arrangements are being made employs Paul's assistance in running her business, "The Latin-American Entertainment Co. Ltd." This, unknown to Paul, is a prostitution agency, and through a complex chain of circumstances he is arrested on the eve of his wedding. Chivalrously shielding Margot, Paul is sentenced to seven years' imprisonment.

Paul is surprisingly happy in prison. "Anyone," he reflects, "who has been to a public school will always feel comparatively at home in prison"—the truth of which is underlined by the reappearance of Prendergast as chaplain and Philbrick and Grimes as prisoners. The chief source of dissatisfaction is the prison governor, Sir Lucas-Dockery, and his cranky theories of penal reform. In the belief that "all crime is due to the repressed desire for aesthetic expression," he supplies a homicidal carpenter with a set of tools with which he beheads the unfortunate Prendergast. Typically, however, the satire on progressive penology is balanced by satire of traditional practice, as represented by the chief warder, a great believer in the Observation Cell:

"That brings out any insanity. I've known several cases of men you could hardly have told were mad—just eccentric, you know—who've been put under observation and after a few days they've been raving lunatics."

Eventually, Margot's friends conspire to move Paul out of prison on the pretext that he needs surgery. At a sanatorium run by Augustus Fagan, M.D., a fake death certificate is composed and Paul is sequestered for a time at Margot's villa on Corfu. There he reencounters Dr. Silenus, the architect of King's Thursday (and a caricature of Walter Gropius), who reads him a lecture on Life. It is, he explains, like the revolving floor of a fairground side show. The nearer you get to the middle the easier it is to keep your balance, and at the very center there is a completely still point, for which Silenus (type of the artist) is searching. Most people, however, are tumbled over and flung about on the perimeter. Some, like Paul, are obviously better off merely watching from a safe seat. Taking this tip, Paul returns, disguised, to resume his studies at Scone College. But he is not quite the same Paul. We leave him studying the history of the Early Church (Gibbon's period, incidentally) in a spirit of intransigent orthodoxy:

There was a bishop in Bithynia, Paul learned, who had denied the Divinity of Christ, the immortality of the soul, the existence of good, the legality of marriage, and the validity of the sacrament of extreme unction! How right they had been to condemn him!

[19]

Vile Bodies is perhaps the most "modern" of all Waugh's novels, both in its fragmentary, *Waste Land*-like construction and in the apocalyptic despair which underlies its brittle comedy. There is a hero—Adam Fenwick-Symes, a slightly more knowing and sophisticated Paul Pennyfeather—but the story of his attempts to obtain enough money to marry his girl, Nina, is only one of many that appear and disappear and reappear in the mosaic of dialogue and description. The brilliant opening chapter, describing a rough Channel crossing, indicates that the novel will distribute its attention widely over the social scene. In quick succession we meet Fr. Rothschild, a caricature of the crafty cosmopolitan Jesuit; the American evangelist Mrs. Melrose Ape and her troupe of "Angels"; Agatha Runcible, Miles Malpractice, and the rest of the Younger Set; the Right Hon. Walter Outrage, "last week's Prime Minister"; two Firbankian dowagers; Adam, aspirant author; and a group of card-playing commercial travelers sufficiently demoralized by the storm to join Fortitude, Chastity, Creative Endeavour, and the rest of Mrs. Ape's angels in her rousing hymn, "There ain't no flies on the Lamb of God."

The novel is saturated in the myth of decline—the decline, for instance, of the British aristocracy:

At Archie Schwert's party the fifteenth Marquess of Vanburgh, Earl Vanburgh de Brendon, Baron Brendon, Lord of the Five Isles and Hereditary Grand Falconer to the Kingdom of Connaught, said to the eighth Earl of Balcairn, Viscount Erdinge, Baron Cairn of Balcairn, Red Knight of Lancaster, Count of the Holy Roman Empire and Chenonceaux Herald to the Duchy of Acquitaine, "Hullo," he said. "Isn't this a repulsive party? What are you going to say about it?" for they were both of them, as it happened, gossip writers for the daily papers.

When Balcairn, excluded from Margot Metroland's party for Mrs. Ape, files a totally invented and outrageously libelous story and puts his head in a gas oven, Adam is offered his job on the *Daily Excess*. He contrives to hold it for a while, first by running a series on "Notable Invalids" and "Titled Eccentrics" (more images of decline), then by inventing fictitious celebrities with whom everyone is soon claiming acquaintance. But Nina, deputizing for him one day, goes too far, and Miles Malpractice becomes the next "Mr. Chatterbox." Opportunities are always circulating in this way in the novel, one man's failure meaning another man's success. Whereas the pattern of events in *Decline and Fall* approximates, eventually, to the benevolent providence of traditional comedy, *Vile Bodies* seems to illustrate the wry judgment expressed in *Labels,* that "Fortune . . . arranges things on the just and rigid system that no-one shall be happy for very long." Adam and Nina, always on the point of getting married, always foiled by some twist of fate, are obvious victims of this system. But the instability of their relationship is also a symptom of what Fr. Rothschild calls "a radical instability in our whole world-order." The Older Generation and the Younger Set are hopelessly alienated. The bankruptcy of politics is represented by Outrage; the bankruptcy of religion, by Mrs. Ape. Economic anarchy is vividly illustrated by Adam's up-and-down financial fortunes.

Returning penniless from France, Adam immediately wins £500 by solving a simple trick with halfpennies, but, being drunk at the time, gives the money to an anonymous Major (also drunk) to put on a horse. The Major places the bet and the horse wins, but though the Major is constantly crossing Adam's path he remains elusive until the very last, apocalyptic scene of the novel, when Adam sits "on a splintered tree stump in the biggest battlefield in the history of the world," by which time galloping inflation has deprived the winnings of any value. In the meantime, Adam is given a check for £1000 by Nina's eccentric father, Colonel Blount, but discovers belatedly that it is signed "Charlie Chaplin." To settle a bill, Adam "sells" Nina to his rival, "Ginger" Littlejohn, for £78-10-2, an episode in which the themes of moral and economic anarchy neatly coincide. The sequel is one of Waugh's most delicate and complex feats of irony. Nina marries Ginger, but he is recalled to his regiment at the end of their honeymoon, and Adam impersonates him when Nina visits her family home. It is Christmas, and to the ritual reception of the new bride is added the traditional celebration of a rustic Christmas. This nostalgic idyll is described appealingly, but is undercut not only by the presence of the adulterous young couple but by the rumors of impending war in the background. The effect of comedy tinged with a strictly controlled pathos is typical of the novel as a whole.

Between 1930 and 1937 Waugh had no permanent home, and traveled extensively, particularly in Africa and Central America. In 1930 he went to Abyssinia to report the coronation of Emperor Haile Selassie I; in 1933 he made an expedition through the hinterland of British Guiana; and in 1935 he returned to Africa to cover the opening phase of the Italian-Abyssinian War for the *Daily Mail*. The curious reader may readily discover for himself in the three travel books, *Remote People* (1931), *Ninety-Two Days* (1934), and *Waugh in Abyssinia* (1936), the sources of characters and incidents in the novels *Black Mischief* (1932), *A Handful of Dust* (1934), and *Scoop* (1938), respectively. *Robbery under Law: The Mexican Object-Lesson* (1939) was more of a political tract than a travelogue, but Waugh used his experience of Mexico in *Brideshead Revisited*.

The spectacle Waugh observed in Africa, of European colonialism and primitive tribalism striving mutually to exploit each other, fed his imagination in a number of ways.

[22]

In the absurdities and incongruities produced by this collision of cultures, the satirist found half his work of distortion and caricature done for him. Only in *Alice in Wonderland* could Waugh find a "parallel for life in Addis Ababa . . . the peculiar flavour of galvanised and translated reality." More seriously, the primitivism of Africa appeared to Waugh as both a foil to and a portent for a "civilization" that was itself declining into a new, and less appealing, kind of barbarism. The racial snobbery of which Waugh has sometimes been accused may, perhaps, be found in his travel books, but not in the corresponding novels, where, if any group survives the author's impartial irony, it is the non-Europeans. The progressive reforms of the Azanian Emperor Seth (in *Black Mischief*) backfire not only upon himself but upon the civilization from which he derives them. His before-and-after posters advocating birth control, for instance, are ironically misconstrued by the natives as promoting a juju for the encouragement of fertility.

Seth personifies a misplaced faith in Western ideas of Progress. When his general, Connolly, defeats a rebel army at the beginning of the novel, Seth does not heed the assurance that the solitary tank on which he had placed all his hopes of victory was useful only as a punishment cell. "We are Progress and the New Age. Nothing can stand in our way." Seth thus falls an easy victim to the opportunism of Basil Seal, a new kind of Waugh hero, or antihero: not the innocent Candide figure, but the innocent cad, a true child of *l'entre-deux-guerres*, so devoid of principle that deception and fraud are reflex responses to him and he is incapable of seeing through his own lies.

Basil collaborates with the Armenian entrepreneur, Mr. Youkoumian, to supply Seth with the apparatus of Progress at a fat percentage, while relaxing amorously with Prudence, the silly daughter of the even sillier English Ambassador. But Seth's delusions of civilized grandeur get out of hand, he is overthrown by a coup, and meets a dark, ambiguous death in the jungle he had despised. In accordance with the same pattern of black comic justice, the idle love-talk of Basil and Prudence ("You're a grand girl, Prudence, and I'd like to eat you." "So you shall, my sweet, anything you want") is gruesomely realized in the dénouement when Basil unwittingly consumes his mistress at a cannibal feast.

Black Mischief is clearly continuous with *Vile Bodies:* there is the same moral atmosphere of deception and corruption, a similarly wide range of representative characters wittily caricatured and deftly juxtaposed through a montage of short scenes, and the same cool, dispassionate irony in the narrator's tone. In *Scoop,* his second African novel, Waugh returned to the ingenuous hero and the circular plot of *Decline and Fall,* while the mainspring of the action—mistaken identity—is a very old comic device indeed. William Boot, the bachelor head of the Boot Magna household, and author of a nature column, "Lush Places," in the *Daily Beast,* is confused with his cousin John Boot, a fashionable novelist, and dispatched by the *Beast*'s proprietor, Lord Copper, to cover an impending war in the African state of "Ishmaelia." There follows much broad but effective satire on the mendacity of journalists and politicians. Though hopelessly unprofessional (while his colleagues are busy inventing spurious news stories, he is sending back long, chatty, and ruinously expensive cables about the weather), William manages to scoop the biggest story of the war and he returns home in triumph. Through a chain of confused circumstances, however, the knighthood and banquet planned for William go to his cousin John and Uncle Theodore, respectively, and William returns gratefully to the peace of Boot Magna and the unexacting composition of "Lush Places." As Europe is to Africa, so the metropolitan world of the *Beast* is to Boot Magna: in both pairings a sophisticated modern barbarism is discomfited by a more intransigent and deeply rooted primitivism. The story of William's expedition to Ishmaelia is bracketed by the baffled attempts of Lord Copper's lackey, Mr. Salter, to control and comprehend William and his rustic environment. Salter's visit to Boot Magna at the end of the novel, for instance, hilariously reenacts the trials and tribulations of jungle exploration.

Between *Black Mischief* and *Scoop* came *A Handful of Dust*, which many critics consider to be Waugh's best novel. What is most striking about it is, perhaps, the way in which the style and technique of Waugh's satirical comedies are effortlessly adapted to a more subtle and soberly realistic treatment of contemporary manners and morals. This is not to say that the novel lacks humor, but the opening line of dialogue, "Was anyone hurt?" strikes an ominous note: many people are to be hurt in this novel. The story is simple in outline. Tony and Brenda Last are apparently an ideally happy couple. She, however, shares halfheartedly in his enthusiasm for his huge, ugly, and expensive property, Hetton Abbey, and drifts into an affair with the vapid man-about-town, John Beaver. The accidental death of the Lasts' only son, also called John, precipitates a crisis, and Brenda asks for a divorce. Tony, after reluctantly cooperating in the undignified preliminaries, is shocked by the threat of losing Hetton into canceling the divorce proceedings. He abruptly embarks on a journey into the Brazilian interior, where he meets a gruesome living death —condemned to read aloud the novels of Dickens to a mad and homicidal settler for the rest of his days. Tony is reported as dead to the outside world; Brenda, suddenly as poor as Beaver, marries Tony's friend Jock Grant-Menzies, and Hetton is converted into a silver-fox farm by an impoverished branch of the family.

Behavior in Waugh's previous novels was the stylized

shadow-play of a general collapse of values. In *A Handful of Dust*, with the abandonment of farce and a movement toward more rounded characterization, the question of individual guilt is raised. Who, then, is responsible for the domestic tragedy it chronicles? There are three principal centers of guilt: John Beaver and the social set to which he parasitically clings, Brenda Last, and Tony himself. Beaver, who "got up at ten and sat near his telephone most of the day, hoping to be rung up," personifies the moral as well as the economic effects of the Great Depression (or Slump, as it was called in Britain), but he is perhaps not as guilty as Brenda's female friends. Her sister, Marjorie, for instance, who encourages the affair at first, disapproves too late and for the wrong, purely snobbish, reasons. Still more sinister is Polly Cockpurse, whose solution to Brenda's problem is to offer Tony a mistress in compensation—the appalling Princess Abdul Akbar. "What *does* the old boy expect," she complains when this experiment fails. "It isn't as though he was everybody's money." The narrator scrupulously avoids comment, allowing these people to condemn themselves out of their own mouths.

Brenda's mixture of adult sophistication and childlike irresponsibility is convincingly presented as both charming and destructive. Her betrayal of Tony is complete and unhesitating, yet curiously devoid of passion or remorse. Tony is the last person to understand what is going on. Even after receiving the letter asking for a divorce, "it was several days before Tony fully realised what it meant. He had got into the habit of loving and trusting Brenda." Yet Waugh skilfully manipulates the reader's sympathies, so that compassion is never entirely withdrawn from Brenda, and Tony's responsibility for the breakdown of the marriage is not overlooked.

Waugh himself said cryptically of *A Handful of Dust* that "it was humanist and contained all I had to say about humanism." What he had to say was largely negative, but entirely implicit. Though Tony is a conscientious churchgoer, religion is, for him, a purely social function, and he is embarrassed by the vicar's condolences on the death of his son: "after all, the last thing one wants to talk about at a time like this is religion." Instead, in a scene of painful comedy, he turns for distraction in this crisis to a game of Animal Snap—one of many examples in Waugh's work of adults regressing to childhood rituals under stress. Tony's real religion is a feudal myth as artificial, as literary, as that of Tennyson's *Idylls of the King*, from which the bedrooms of Hetton are named (Brenda, of course, sleeps in "Guinevere," and Beaver in "Lancelot"). Tony's cult of Hetton is an index of his culpable ignorance of objective good and evil. When he finally grasps the nature of the world he lives in, "A whole Gothic world had come to grief. . . . There was now no armour glittering through the forest glades, no embroidered feet on the green sward; the cream and dappled unicorns had fled." Yet still Tony is haunted by his myth. The Lost City which he seeks in the depths of Brazil is not a real city, still less the City of God, but a transfigured Hetton: "He had a clear picture of it in his mind. It was Gothic in character, all vanes and pinnacles." At last, in the delirium of fever, he tells the settler, Mr. Todd, "what I have learned in the forest. . . . There is no City, Mrs Beaver has covered it with chromium plating and converted it into flats." There are, however, in the forest the "Victorian Gothic" novels of Dickens.

The title is, of course, taken from *The Waste Land:* "I will show you fear in a handful of dust." The novel depicts a sick society whose hedonism disintegrates at the first touch of mortality. Crucial, here, is the bitterly ironic scene in which Brenda, informed of her son's death, confuses his name with Beaver's. But Waugh does not, in the cause-and-effect style of the Victorian novel, logically connect the child's death with the mother's wrongdoing. "Every one agreed that it was nobody's fault." It was nobody's fault, we are made to feel, because, like the broken marriage, it was everybody's fault.

In 1936 Waugh's own marriage was annulled by Rome and he was free to marry again. He did so in the following year, and settled down with his wife Laura in a sixteenth-century Gloucestershire manor where, in due course, he raised a family of six children. The advantages of domestic stability, however, seem, as far as Waugh's writing was concerned, to have been more than offset by the unsettling political climate of the late thirties, and by certain changes within Waugh himself. The unfinished *Work Suspended* (1942), the principal product of these years, seems suggestive in this respect. It is the first-person narrative of John Plant, an expatriate writer of successful detective stories who, returning to England on the death of his father, finds he no longer has any inclination to finish the book he is working on. Instead he desultorily searches for a house in the country and develops an obsessive but undeclared passion for the pregnant wife of a friend. We are given a delightful, affectionately ironic portrait of John's father, a studiously unfashionable painter, and glimpses of a promising comic character called Atwater, before the first air-raid sirens of World War II bring the story, and "an epoch—my epoch," to an abrupt and inconclusive end. Several features of *Work Suspended* anticipate later developments in Waugh's fiction, especially in *Brideshead Revisited:* the autobiographical convention, the slower, more ruminative tempo of the prose, inclining toward long and elaborately constructed analogies, and the pervasive tone of a narrator who feels sardonically alienated from his society and threatened by apathy and ennui within himself.

[28]

In his next novel, however, Waugh returned to the mode and the cast of his earlier comedies, following the fortunes of Basil Seal and a host of other familiar figures through the first year of the war, "that odd, dead period before the Churchillian Renaissance," as the Dedication says, "which people called at the time the Great Bore War." Though *Put Out More Flags* (1942) certainly has its moments (Basil Seal's racket with evacuees, for instance, or the bomb-carrying lunatic in the War Office) the novel has neither structural nor thematic unity. The satirical impulse pulls against a patriotic one, in accordance with which the aging Bright Young Things—even Basil Seal—are shown as finally undergoing, in the national emergency, an implausible change of heart (an organ which, in the past, they showed few signs of possessing). But one should not judge *Put Out More Flags* too harshly, for it was written on a troopship, partly to relieve the author's own boredom.

It was entirely characteristic of Waugh that at the outbreak of war he enlisted in the Royal Marines, subsequently joining the first Commandos. He was thus one of the few important British writers of his generation to have firsthand experience of regimental life and active service, and this was to bear fruit in his trilogy about the war. Fortunately, perhaps, for English letters, an injury sustained late in 1943 prevented him from taking part in the Normandy landings; and it was during the ensuing convalescent leave that he wrote *Brideshead Revisited*, published in 1945.

This novel, he drily remarked in the Preface to the revised edition of 1960, "lost me such esteem as I once enjoyed among my contemporaries, and led me into an unfamiliar world of fan mail and press photographers." It was his first really popular success, especially in America, where sales reached three quarters of a million copies; but in the more select circles of literary opinion it dismayed admirers of his early work, such as Edmund Wilson. The most just assessment of the novel is Waugh's own Preface, where he shows himself fully aware of its structural faults and the excesses and false notes of its language. The latter he attributes partly to the time and place of the novel's composition:

It was a bleak period of present privation and threatening disaster . . . and in consequence the book is informed with a kind of gluttony, for food and wine, for the splendours of the recent past, and for rhetorical and ornamental language, which now with a full stomach I find distasteful. . . . It is offered to a younger generation of readers as a souvenir of the Second War rather than of the twenties or of the thirties, with which it ostensibly deals.

Brideshead Revisited is indeed a classic example of the literary taste of the forties, and for this reason one may doubt the wisdom of Waugh's attempts to temper its "gluttony" in the revised edition. It was also Waugh's first—and, essentially, his last—contribution to the "Catholic Novel." This fictional tradition, which goes back to the French Decadence, is characteristically concerned with the operation of God's grace in the world, with a conflict between secular and divine values in which the latter are usually allowed an ironic and unexpected triumph. The theme which François Mauriac explored in his bleak French provinces, and Graham Greene in various seedy backwaters of civilization, Waugh embodied in the story of an English aristocratic family, filtering it through a narrator whose humbler background dramatizes the glamorous appeal—even in its decline—of hereditary privilege, and whose gradually eroded agnosticism acts as a buffer between the skeptical reader and the religious values endorsed by the author. The double-sidedness of the novel's concern is indicated by its deliberately old-fashioned subtitle: "The Sacred and Profane Memories of Captain Charles Ryder."

The frame of the main narrative is a completely convincing account of how Charles Ryder, an embittered regimental officer who has already resigned himself to a war of inglorious tedium, moves one night into a new billet which, by morning, reveals itself as the house of Brideshead, a place associated with the most thrilling and painful moments of his past. His memory released by this spring (the whole novel is heavily Proustian in feeling), Ryder begins to recall the history of his connections with the Brideshead family: Lord Marchmain, who adopted the Catholic faith of his wife, then apostasized and deserted her to live in sin and social disgrace with his Italian mistress; Lady Marchmain, a woman of great piety, but destructive possessiveness; and their children—"Bridey," the dull, dim eldest son; the exquisite and enigmatic Julia; the feckless and charming Sebastian; and plain, loyal Cordelia. It is through Sebastian that Ryder first becomes involved with this family, when they are both gay, irresponsible undergraduates at Oxford in the early twenties.

Oxford—submerged now and obliterated, irrecoverable as Lyonnesse, so quickly have the waters come flooding in—Oxford, in those days was still a city of aquatint. In her spacious and quiet streets men walked and spoke as they had done in Newman's day; her autumnal mists, her grey springtime, and the rare glory of her summer days—such as that day—when the chestnut was in flower and the bells rang out high and clear over her gables and cupolas, exhaled the soft vapours of a thousand years of learning.

Clearly, through the medium of Ryder, Waugh's style has lost some of its classical control and modern terseness, and a certain relaxation and lushness has crept in: semicolons and parentheses break up the syntactical structure to make room for adjectival and adverbial phrases heavy with sensation, with aesthetic and emotive self-indulgence. "This was my conversion to the baroque," says Ryder, of his introduction to the house of Brideshead, and the conversion is reflected in his prose.

A nostalgic lyricism permeates the first, long section of the novel, "Et in Arcadia Ego"; but two finely drawn characters, Mr. Ryder, Sr. and the homosexual aesthete Anthony Blanche, who vainly warns Charles against the fatal "charm" of the Brideshead family, strike a welcome note of skepticism and irony. The narrative is mainly concerned with Sebastian's decline from youthful dissipation to a deliberate and rather obscurely motivated alcoholism, so that Ryder finds himself painfully divided between his loyalty to his friend and his attachment to the rest of the family. Eventually Sebastian is abandoned as a hopeless case and left to live in exile; but Charles, rather unfairly, is also banished from Brideshead by Lady Marchmain. She now has another cross to bear in the marriage of Julia to the Canadian Rex Mottram, a brash and vulgar man-on-the-make whose instruction in the Catholic faith (the occasion of some amusing theological farce) is abruptly terminated by Bridey's discovery that he is a divorcé. Lady Marchmain dies, the family's London home is sold and demolished to make way for an apartment block, and Brideshead itself is almost deserted.

Ryder picks up his story ten years later, when he is returning to England from a painting tour of Mexico. In the meantime he has married and become a successful, though unfashionable, artist, best known for his portfolios of fine domestic architecture. His wife, who, we gather, has been unfaithful to him, and for whom he no longer feels any affection, joins him in New York for the voyage to England. On the same liner is Julia, now quite disillusioned in her own marriage, and in the course of a violent storm, which incapacitates nearly all the other passengers, she and Charles become lovers. Ryder's quiet but deadly hatred of his wife and the world of false, vulgar luxury (epitomized by the liner) which she inhabits is extremely well rendered; and so, in its way, is the high romance of the storm. Charles and Julia set about getting divorced preparatory to marriage, and when the ailing Lord Marchmain hints that he may bequeath Brideshead to them the ultimate "profane" dream of Charles Ryder seems about to come true. The sacred, however, has already disturbed the even tenor of his relationship with Julia, when a casual remark of Bridey's reawakens her Catholic sense of sin; and when Lord Marchmain returns to Brideshead to die and, against all expectation, is reconciled to the Church with his last breath, Julia returns to her Faith and separates from Charles. There are several hints that Ryder himself is later converted in consequence of these events; and, as so often in modern Catholic literature (one thinks, for instance, of Francis Thompson's *The Hound of Heaven*), the descent of God's grace, because of the human sacrifice it demands, has an aspect of catastrophe—here conveyed through the iterative image of an avalanche.

The flaws of style and structure Waugh himself noted become more obvious the more often *Brideshead* is revisited. The book is quite unbalanced by the long and leisurely treatment of the young Sebastian, who then drops almost entirely out of the picture. Rather clumsy secondhand reports of his progress to an unorthodox kind of sanctity, and the attempt to identify him as the "forerunner" of Charles's passion for Julia, do not solve this problem. The elegiac realism that is the narrator's staple style is disturbed at times by passages written in quite different and discordant registers—for instance, the stylized caricature of Rex's circle, or Julia's long aria on the subject of sin. The extended images—the avalanche of grace, Sebastian as a Polynesian Islander—though elaborated with elegance and beauty, seem drawn from literary stereotypes rather than experience. But what has most offended readers hostile to *Brideshead Revisited* is the narrator's generously indulged spleen against the democratization of English society in his lifetime, a development epitomized for him by his plebeian brother-officer, Hooper. Ryder's reflection on Lady Marchmain's three gallant brothers, killed in World War I, has become notorious:

These men must die to make a world for Hooper; they were the aborigines, vermin by right of law, to be shot off at leisure so that things might be safe for the travelling salesman, with his polygonal pince-nez, his fat wet handshake, his grinning dentures.

As I indicated earlier, the epilogue leaves Ryder resigned, in his adopted faith, to the passing of Brideshead as he knew it, but this comes too late to erase the impression that in this novel Waugh's myth of decline has become damagingly fixed and limited to a particular phase and a partial view of modern social history.

In his next full-length novel, Waugh turned to a quite new subject, potentially a much more affirmative one than anything he had attempted previously; but the interesting thing is how little difference it seems to make. *Helena* (1950) is a fictionalized biography of the saint who, according to the legend Waugh chooses to follow, was the daughter of a British chieftain (Waugh makes him King Coel, or Cole, of nursery rhyme fame) and the mother of the Emperor Constantine, before she discovered, in her old age, the relics of the True Cross in Jerusalem. The overt purpose of the novel is to honor St. Helena, and through her to emphasize the historicity of the Incarnation and the common-sense reasonableness of Christian revelation; yet this message comes across less forcefully than the oblique comments on modern life. Though the novel was obviously thoroughly researched, the characterization and dialogue are deliberately, anachronistically modern, thus underlining the thinly disguised parallels between the fourth and twentieth centuries: both periods in which a great Empire began to crumble and confusion reigned in politics, manners, and morals. Waugh even contrives to insert satire on modern architecture and nonrepresentational art into this historical novel.

Since the period was one in which Christianity emerged from the catacombs and began to impose its values on European civilization, it might have been expected that in *Helena* Waugh would at last put aside his myth of decline. There is, indeed, a passage celebrating the "springtide" of Christianity: "New green life was pricking and unfolding and entwining everywhere among the masonry and ruts." Yet almost at once the narrator qualifies this optimistic note, undercutting the enthusiasm of the Christians, questioning the significance of Constantine's "conversion," and pointing out that subsequently "the oblivious Caesars fought on." The perfect union of the sacred and profane is as far from historical realization as it ever is in Waugh's vision. Even Helena's discovery of the Cross carries with it the penalty of inevitable human abuse:

She saw the sanctuaries of Christendom become a fairground, stalls hung with beads and medals, substances yet unknown pressed into sacred emblems; heard a chatter of haggling in tongues yet unspoken. She saw the treasuries of the Church filled with forgeries and impostures. She saw Christians fighting and stealing to get possession of trash.

Between *Brideshead Revisited* and *Helena* Waugh published two short satirical novels. In *Scott-King's Modern Europe* (1947), a classics teacher at an English public school makes an uncomfortable visit to a corrupt central European republic and is confirmed in his opinion that "it would be very wicked indeed to do anything to fit a boy for the modern world."

[35]

There are some amusing episodes, but on the whole it is a rather tired piece of work. *The Loved One* (1948) is a much more effective attack on the modern world—a world that was becoming increasingly Americanized. When Waugh went to Hollywood in 1947 to discuss the filming of *Brideshead Revisited*, the project was abandoned because of his intransigence over the script, but he found fresh inspiration in Forest Lawn, the great cemetery of Los Angeles. In "Whispering Glades" (thus, thinly disguised and with little exaggeration, Forest Lawn appears in the novel)—where the fear in a handful of dust is assuaged by vulgar ostentation and gross materialism, where the features of the "Loved Ones" are improved by cosmetics and wrenched into consoling expressions before they are expensively entombed among debased replicas of classical art and architecture—Waugh found a rich and many-faceted symbol for the denaturing of human life in the twentieth century. The novel is packed with images of natural order inverted or perverted: "the poulterer's pinch" the mortician Mr. Joyboy gives to his corpses, the empty beehives humming electronically on the "Lake Isle of Innisfree," Kaiser's Stoneless Peaches. Whereas the buildings on the movie-lots look solid and are in fact two-dimensional, those in Whispering Glades have the reverse, but equally unnatural effect.

The plot is a black comic variation on Henry James's International Theme: European Decadence, in the person of Dennis Barlow, a young British poet, is allowed to triumph over an innocent but depraved America, represented by Mr. Joyboy and, in part, by his assistant Aimée Thanatogenos. When Dennis's career as a script-writer is abruptly terminated, he takes a job at the Happier Hunting Ground, a pets' mortuary modeled on Whispering Glades. The suicide of another expatriate Englishman brings him to the great original in a mood of ironic homage. Here he meets Aimée, a girl in whom, though she has the same mass-produced good looks as all the other girls Dennis meets, he recognizes a hidden kindred spirit: "sole Eve in a hygienic Eden, this girl was a decadent." While feeding his imagination on the sublime absurdities of Whispering Glades, Dennis courts Aimée with poems copied unscrupulously from the *Oxford Book of English Verse*. Mr. Joyboy asserts his rival claims on her affections. Hopelessly divided between an atavistic attraction to the "unethical" Dennis, and her conditioned respect and admiration for Joyboy, Aimée Thanatogenos (whose name, of course, signifies love and death) commits suicide in circumstances highly compromising to Joyboy. For a financial consideration Dennis cremates Aimée's corpse in the ovens of the Happier Hunting Ground. No tincture of emotion clouds the distilled irony of this novella.

He entered the office and made a note in the book kept there for that purpose. Tomorrow and on every anniversary as long as the Happier Hunting Ground existed a postcard would go to Mr Joyboy. *Your little Aimée is wagging her tail in heaven tonight, thinking of you.*

In 1952 Waugh published *Men at Arms*, the first volume of a projected trilogy about World War II. The second volume, *Officers and Gentlemen*, followed in 1955, with a note that the work was concluded. Fortunately, however, Waugh reverted to his original scheme and published the third volume, *Unconditional Surrender*, in 1961. In the intervening years he wrote a conscientious, but rather low-spirited biography of his friend Mgr. Ronald Knox (1959) and a travel book, *A Tourist in Africa* (1960). *The Ordeal of Gilbert Pinfold* (1957) is easily the most interesting product of these years, which were evidently difficult ones for its author. This highly confessional novella was quite unexpected, coming as it did from a writer notorious for the fierce defense of his privacy, who rebuffed research students, sued journalists, and liked to be photographed at home standing defiantly beside the notices *Entrée Interdite aux Promeneurs* and "No Admittance on Business." It describes, essentially, a nervous breakdown, exacerbated by the imprudent use of drugs. Just how close the story was to Waugh's own experience can be verified from Frances Donaldson's memoir, *Evelyn Waugh: Portrait of a Country Neighbour;* but no reader could fail to see in the opening chapter, "Portrait of the Artist in Middle Age," a revealing and far from uncritical self-portrait.

Mr. Pinfold, finding that increasing doses of chloral and bromide are not arresting the deterioration of his health and spirits, or loosening his writer's block, embarks on a ship bound for Ceylon. In his cabin he is disconcerted to overhear, apparently by an acoustic freak, the voices of some other passengers abusing his good name and plotting his humiliation. Mr. Pinfold is unable to trace these voices, but he finds them totally, appallingly authentic even when their activities take a wildly melodramatic turn, involving murder, torture, and conspiracy. Pinfold is, of course, the victim of hallucinations; but he does not concede this possibility until the end of the story when, refusing a bargain of peace in return for secrecy offered by his tormenting voices, he discusses them openly with his wife and doctor. What is fascinating about the hallucinations is that they are "displaced" and distorted projections of Mr. Pinfold-Waugh's public and private life. Some of the accusations he receives are absurd, some have a specious plausibility, and some—perhaps the majority—are criticisms Mr. Pinfold-Waugh has, on occasion, directed at others; for example, "Mr Pinfold typified the decline of England, of rural England in particular. He was a reincarnation . . . of the 'new men' of the Tudor period who had despoiled the Church and the peasantry." The "ordeal" is therefore a kind of identity crisis and the writing up of the experience a therapeutic exercise in self-analysis. That the myth of decline should be so pointedly turned upon its author is a measure of the detachment Waugh achieved, and the gain can be clearly seen in the completion of the war trilogy, where the somewhat affected and irritable toryism of Waugh's later years is tempered by a mature irony and compassion.

Nearly all novels about World War II are antiwar novels, but the note of protest is rarely supported by any coherent structure of ideas, and is usually compromised by the atavistic gusto with which bloodshed and combat are described. *Sword of Honour* (as Waugh's trilogy is collectively entitled) makes a political and moral judgment on the war which, though debatable, is thoughtful and telling; and its treatment of soldiering is consistently ironic and antiheroic. The story is long and complicated, but more than narrative continuity binds the three novels together: each has a dominant comic antihero who parodies or inverts the hero's stance, and each ends with an anticlimactic "battle" which confirms the hero's disillusionment.

The hero is Guy Crouchback—a name that combines associations of the reckless and ineffectual Catholic conspirator, Guy Fawkes, of the stooped Don Quixote, and of Christ bowed under the Cross. The imitation of Christ, however, is more evident in Mr. Crouchback, Sr.; in Guy himself, though he is loyal to his Catholic faith, spirituality has dried up along with human emotion. It is partly to redeem his hollow life that, at the age of thirty-five, childless and deserted by his wife, he closes up his Italian *castello* and, in a mood of quixotic chivalry, returns to England to enlist in the war that is just beginning. There is also an ideological motive: for the deeply conservative Guy, the Nazi-Soviet pact of 1939 has suddenly simplified the complexities of interwar politics:

Now, splendidly, everything had become clear. The enemy at last was plain in view, huge and hateful, all disguise cast off. It was the

Modern Age in arms. Whatever the outcome there was a place for him in that battle.

Guy's disillusionment begins almost at once. No one in England seems to share his indignation at the Russian invasion of Poland, and no one seems to want him in the Army. Eventually Guy obtains a commission in the unfashionable but proudly traditional regiment of Halberdiers. In the activity of training and the camaraderie of the mess, it seems to Guy that he is "experiencing something he had missed in boyhood, a happy adolescence." As the novel proceeds, this analogy is more and more ironically developed. Thus Guy's first "war-wound" is a wrenched knee sustained in the course of an improvised football game at a rowdy regimental dinner. The Halberdiers are later billeted in a school whose dormitories are named after battles in World War I, and here "the preparatory school way of life was completely recreated." Brigadier Ritchie-Hook, the hideously scarred, legendary veteran of that war ("where lesser men collected helmets, Ritchie-Hook once came back from a raid across no-man's-land with the dripping head of a German sentry in either hand"), arouses in Guy a hero worship whimsically nourished by memories of the intrepid Truslove, a military hero of his boyhood reading.

Guy's antitype, or Jungian "shadow," in *Men at Arms* is Apthorpe, a fine comic character in whom, as Frederick Stopp has shown, the traditional *miles gloriosus* is crossed with a whole line of pseudo-respectable good fellows in Waugh's fiction. Apthorpe, like Guy, is older than most of the recruits, and the two men naturally become companions and rivals. At first Apthorpe, who makes great play with his experience in the tropics, cuts an impressive figure, but the speciousness of his pretensions is amusingly betrayed by beautifully managed nuances of speech and gesture. Apthorpe becomes involved in an extended feud with Ritchie-Hook over the use of his treasured "thunderbox" (a portable field latrine), an object surrounded by such mystery and intrigue that a fascist spy reports it as a secret weapon. Guy is drawn into the feud, an action which underlines the approximation of his military career to schoolboy pranks rather than serious warfare. Real combat, when it comes, is scarcely less bathetic. After endless delays "Hookforce" sails to West Africa to mount an assault on the Vichy French in Dakar. The operation is canceled at the last moment, but Ritchie-Hook proposes a small night-reconnaissance expedition which Guy volunteers to lead ("This was the true Truslove spirit"). Unknown to Guy, Ritchie-Hook has concealed himself in the party and endangers their lives and the mission when he plunges into the jungle to decapitate a Negro sentry. Guy's reputation is unfairly blemished by this absurd escapade; and when, a little later, he imprudently takes the hospitalized Apthorpe a bottle of whisky with which the old fraud finally kills himself, Guy is sent back to England in some disgrace. Thus ends *Men at Arms*.

Two other characters must be mentioned. One is Virginia Troy, Guy's wife, but twice remarried and now again on the loose. Guy, in a passing mood of lechery, turns to Virginia on the casuistical grounds that she is still his wife in the eyes of God, and is quite rightly rebuffed. The other character is Trimmer, hairdresser on a transatlantic liner in prewar days, a disreputable opportunist who is commissioned in the Halberdiers but quickly transferred. In *Officers and Gentlemen* circumstances bring both Guy and Trimmer together again on the remote Scottish isle of Mugg, where a commando unit is being rapidly decimated by the rigors of its training. Posing as a major, Trimmer has a brief affair with Virginia at a Glasgow hotel, and develops a maudlin passion from which Virginia finds it difficult to free herself. For Trimmer, grotesquely, is chosen to lead Operation Popgun, a mission designed by the press officer Ian Kilbannock to provide the nation with a proletarian hero. The objective—a disused and unguarded lighthouse off the island of Jersey—is entirely pointless. Because of a navigation error, however, the party lands on the mainland of occupied France, and in a scene of fine burlesque the terrified Trimmer and the eloquently drunk Kilbannock stumble around in the dark while their men contrive to blow up a railway line. This fiasco is converted by Kilbannock's invention into a feat of great daring, and Trimmer finds himself the hero of the British public. By enjoying Guy's wife and travestying his dreams of military glory, Trimmer thus takes over from Apthorpe the function of ironic antihero. Guy, meanwhile, has had a long and tedious journey round the Cape to Egypt, arriving just in time to participate in the British withdrawal from Crete. The ignominy, misery, and confusion of this debacle, which Waugh himself experienced, are rendered in his finest piece of realistic writing. "Hookforce" is left to surrender to the Germans, but at the last moment Guy jumps into a small open boat from which, after many days, he is carried to safety by another escaper, Corporal Major Ludovic. This, in every sense of the word, queer man is compiling a book of Pensées, some of which are disconcertingly apt: "Captain Crouchback . . . would like to believe that the war is being fought by [gentlemen]. But all gentlemen are now very old." He is also the batman of Ivor Clare, a dashing young Commando officer who has seemed to Guy to represent "quintessential England, the man Hitler had not taken into account." Recovering from his ordeal in Alexandria, however, Guy learns that Clare deserted his men in Crete, though the intriguing socialite Julia Stitch (an old face from *Scoop*) is successfully covering his traces. This betrayal, combined with an earlier unpleasant experience in the confessional and the news of Germany's invasion of Russia (which, by the unprincipled logic of war, makes Britain the ally of Communist tyranny), completes Guy's disillusionment in his crusade:

He was back after less than two years' pilgrimage in a Holy Land of illusion in the old ambiguous world, where priests were spies and gallant friends proved traitors and his country was led blundering into dishonour.

The sequel, *Unconditional Surrender*, does not modify—if anything, it deepens—Guy's skepticism about the aims of the war; but he does attain a more positive, mature, and humble perspective on his own part in it. Guy is selected, in droll circumstances, to join a British military mission to the Yugoslavian partisans. First he is sent for parachute training to an establishment weirdly administered by Ludovic, now promoted Major for his apparent heroism in the escape from Crete. Crazed with guilt about two murders committed on that occasion, which he mistakenly thinks Guy knows about, Ludovic emerges in this novel as the comic shadow of the hero. Eventually he publishes a successful romantic novel about the aristocracy (which incidentally bears a parodic resemblance to *Brideshead Revisited*) and with the royalties buys Guy's Italian *castello*. Guy is injured in a practice parachute drop and, while convalescing in London, is sought out by Virginia, now horrified to discover that she is pregnant by Trimmer. To legitimatize the child, Guy takes Virginia back as his wife, and both find the arrangement unexpectedly comfortable. Guy's generous gesture, condemned by his friends as quixotically chivalrous, is in fact of all his actions the least deserving of such a criticism. In Yugoslavia, Guy learns that Virginia has been killed by a flying bomb, but the child lives on, a living symbol of Guy's (and Waugh's?) modified class consciousness.

In the Yugoslavian episode (closely based, like most of the

[43]

others, on Waugh's personal experience) the critique of Allied policy as cooperation in the "'dismemberment of Christendom'" is forcefully underlined. The Communist partisans are portrayed as crafty, repressive, and not particularly effective. A rather specious "battle" is arranged to impress a visiting team of Allied top brass, amongst whom Ritchie-Hook reappears. Of course he cannot resist the opportunity to "biff the enemy" and dies a grotesque, vainglorious death, useless to all except the partisans, whose faces he saves. Impotent in matters of large policy, Guy takes a small stand on behalf of a group of Jewish displaced persons who are being ill-treated by the partisans. He has very moderate success, and unknowingly contributes to the judicial murder of their leader, Mme Kanyi. In his last interview with her there is a very moving moment of truth which casts a piercing illumination back upon the whole story of Guy Crouchback's war. "Is there any place that is free from evil?" Mme Kanyi asks.

"It is too simple to say that only the Nazis wanted war. These communists wanted it too. . . . Many of my people wanted it. . . . It seems to me that there was a will to war, a death wish, everywhere. Even good men thought their private honour would be satisfied by war. They could assert their manhood by killing and being killed. They would accept hardship in recompense for having been selfish and lazy. Danger justified privilege. I knew Italians . . . who felt this. Were there none in England?"

"God forgive me," said Guy. "I was one of them."

I have given only a skeletal outline of *Sword of Honour*, omitting dozens of memorable characters and episodes. At first, it seems to have the structure of picaresque fiction, in which the only principle of unity is the hero, moving through a linear sequence of diverse adventures. But on closer acquaintance one is impressed by the way in which Waugh contains the proliferating growth of his story within a fine mesh of cross reference and recurrence. Time after time, characters whom we have not expected to see again pop up once more in circumstances at once surprising and ironically fitting. The absurd obsession of Colonel Grace-Groundling-Marchpole, an Intelligence Officer who fits every piece of information that comes through his hands into one vast global conspiracy, parodies the author's own controlling vision. Waugh's mature style, more measured and subdued than that of the early comedies, more disciplined and self-denying than that of *Brideshead Revisited*, is a flexible medium which allows him to move effortlessly between the comic and the serious.

Sword of Honour has gradually won recognition as the most distinguished British novel to come out of World War II: no other work has approached its grasp of the multiple ironies —some absurd, some tragic and terrible—of that war. It thus made a fitting climax to Waugh's literary career, in assessing which we are probably driven back upon the "placing" of Mr. Pinfold. Measured against the very great novelists, whether of the nineteenth century or the twentieth, Waugh falls a little short of the first rank. But almost everything he wrote displayed the integrity of a master craftsman, and much of it was touched with comic genius. His best novels will bear infinite rereading, and still retain their power to reduce the solitary reader to tears of helpless laughter. That is a rare and elusive gift.

SELECTED BIBLIOGRAPHY

NOTE: *Only first English and American editions of Waugh's works are listed, except where later editions are of special interest. Most of Waugh's fiction is published in a Uniform Edition by Chapman & Hall, London, and many titles are available in paperback editions, published mainly by Penguin in England and by Dell in the United States.*

Principal Works of Evelyn Waugh

Rossetti: His Life and Works. London, Duckworth, 1928; New York, Dodd, Mead, 1928.

Decline and Fall. London, Chapman & Hall, 1928; New York, Farrar & Rinehart, 1929.

Vile Bodies. London, Chapman & Hall, 1930; New York, Cape & Smith, 1930.

Labels: A Mediterranean Journal. London, Duckworth, 1930; New York, Cape & Smith, 1930 (under the title, A Bachelor Abroad: A Mediterranean Journal).

Remote People. London, Duckworth, 1931; New York, Farrar & Rinehart, 1932 (under the title, They Were Still Dancing).

Black Mischief. London, Chapman & Hall, 1932; New York, Farrar & Rinehart, 1932.

Ninety-Two Days. London, Duckworth, 1934; New York, Farrar & Rinehart, 1934.

A Handful of Dust. London, Chapman & Hall, 1934; New York, Farrar & Rinehart, 1934.

Edmund Campion. London, Sheed & Ward, 1935; Boston, Little, Brown, 1946.

Mr. Loveday's Little Outing, and Other Sad Stories. London, Chapman & Hall, 1936; Boston, Little, Brown, 1936.

Scoop. London, Chapman & Hall, 1938; Boston, Little, Brown, 1938.

Robbery under Law: The Mexican Object-Lesson. London, Chapman & Hall, 1939; Boston, Little, Brown, 1939 (under the title, Mexico; An Object-Lesson).

Work Suspended. London, Chapman & Hall, 1942. (See Tactical Exercise, below.)

Put Out More Flags. London, Chapman & Hall, 1942; Boston, Little, Brown, 1942.

Brideshead Revisited. London, Chapman & Hall, 1945; Boston,

Little, Brown, 1945. Revised ed., London, Chapman & Hall, 1960.

When the Going Was Good (selections from earlier travel books). London, Duckworth, 1946; Boston, Little, Brown, 1946.

Scott-King's Modern Europe. London, Chapman & Hall, 1947; Boston, Little, Brown, 1949.

The Loved One. London, Chapman & Hall, 1948; Boston, Little, Brown, 1948.

Helena. London, Chapman & Hall, 1950; Boston, Little, Brown, 1950.

Men at Arms. London, Chapman & Hall, 1952; Boston, Little, Brown, 1952.

Love among the Ruins. London, Chapman & Hall, 1953. (See Tactical Exercise, below.)

Tactical Exercise. Boston, Little, Brown, 1954. (Includes Work Suspended and Love among the Ruins.)

Officers and Gentlemen. London, Chapman & Hall, 1955; Boston, Little, Brown, 1955.

The Ordeal of Gilbert Pinfold. London, Chapman & Hall, 1957; Boston, Little, Brown, 1957.

Ronald Knox. London, Chapman & Hall, 1959; Boston, Little, Brown, 1959.

Unconditional Surrender. London, Chapman & Hall, 1961; Boston, Little, Brown, 1962 (under the title, The End of the Battle).

A Little Learning. London, Chapman & Hall, 1964; Boston, Little, Brown, 1964.

Sword of Honour. (One-volume ed.) London, Chapman & Hall, 1965.

Critical Works and Commentary

Bergonzi, Bernard. "Evelyn Waugh's Gentlemen," *Critical Quarterly*, V (1963), 23–36.

Bradbury, Malcolm. Evelyn Waugh. Edinburgh and London, Oliver & Boyd, 1964.

Carens, James F. The Satiric Art of Evelyn Waugh. Seattle and London, University of Washington Press, 1966.

De Vitis, A. A. Roman Holiday: The Catholic Novels of Evelyn Waugh. New York, Bookman Associates, 1956.

Donaldson, Frances. Evelyn Waugh: Portrait of a Country Neighbour. London, Weidenfeld & Nicolson, 1967.

Dyson, A. E. "Evelyn Waugh and the Mysteriously Disappearing Hero," *Critical Quarterly*, II (1960), 72–79.

Greenblatt, Stephen Jay. Three Modern Satirists: Waugh, Huxley and Orwell. New Haven, Yale University Press, 1965.

Jebb, Julian. "Evelyn Waugh: An Interview," *Paris Review*, VIII (1963), 73–85.

Kermode, Frank. "Mr. Waugh's Cities," in Puzzles and Epiphanies, pp. 164–75. London, Routledge, 1962.

O'Donnell, Donat (Conor Cruise O'Brien). Maria Cross: Imaginative Patterns in a Group of Modern Catholic Writers. London, Chatto & Windus, 1953.

Stopp, Frederick J. Evelyn Waugh: Portrait of an Artist. London, Chapman & Hall, 1958.

Waugh, Alec. My Brother Evelyn and Other Profiles. London, Cassell, 1968.

Wilson, Edmund. "Never Apologize, Never Explain: The Art of Evelyn Waugh," and "Splendors and Miseries of Evelyn Waugh," in Classics and Commercials. New York, Farrar, Straus, 1950.